Black Rose, Dying

A collection of poetry

Edward Val

With introduction by award-winning
poet and author Mark Orrin

$\mathcal{LOSP}$

Lost Soulz Press
Melbourne, Florida

Lost Soulz Press
An imprint of Veterans Publishing Company
3655 Suncrest Drive
Melbourne, FL 32904
www.veteranspublishing.com

ISBN-13: 978-0692999400
ISBN-10: 069299940X

Book Design: Edward Val

Printed in the United States of America

Dedication

This book is dedicated to all the world's Lost Souls
trying to make their ways.
In this darkness may you one day find light and meaning.

In memory of...

May this book evoke the memory of the many soldiers who have died serving their country during these bleak times.

As the Hammer Falls:

As the hammer falls,
spraying searing lead.
Another innocent soul lies wounded,
another innocent soul lies dead.
A victim of random violence
Frequent in our world today
So pause and give silence
For the life thread;
that so tragically flew away.
Kneel and pray,
battle the passionless feelings and gray.
Strive for a brighter future,
but never forget the loss
On that bitter July day.

In Memory of
Nikkiana Seals Jones

August 13, 1981—July 24, 2009

Contents

Part Three: Fall, 35

Part Four: Winter, 59

Introduction

By Mark Orrin, M.A.
Award-Winning Author/Poet

With *Black Rose, Dying*, his eloquent, four-season-spanning, tour-de-force collection of poems, Edward Val (E'Val) joins the honored ranks of war-haunted poets who include Britain's Sir Walter Raleigh, Wilfred Owen, and Siegfried Sassoon, and America's Stephen Crane and James Dickey.

E'Val comes by his warrior status authentically and gravely: Born in Camden, N.J., in early 1983, E'Val has survived four Army deployments as an infantryman. One in Afghanistan and three in Iraq; wounded in combat, he's received a Purple Heart and lost many friends and brothers to battles' ravages. As a wordsmith, he's published a previous poetry collection, *Enlightened Heart/Darkened Soul*; at this moment, he's working on a third book of poems and a novel to be titled *Of Tooth and Nail*. Personally, E'Val is a father and a man of art and passion who wishes to create in all facets of his life and effect change in his world by his words – which he wields in startling variety.

E'Val's poetry in *Black Rose, Dying* ranges widely in forms and themes, from free to rhyming and off-rhyming verse to Haiku to several brief prose poems, rendered with terse wit, irony and probing clarity. "Truth" is suffused with a wry brevity that indeed reminds one of Stephen Crane. "Haiku 2" distills Dickey's observation (in his "Firebombing") that death can spread in bleak beauty. "A Soldier's Tears" shares the poet's wrenching regret for the unavoidable yet tragic "collateral damage" a soldier deals in the "line of duty."

"Me and You" reflects the ambiguity of pain in parting from a loved one to go and make war. "Rant" assails a love-betrayer in stark imagery. "True Love" – does this poem deconstruct a myth... or depict a reality one irresistibly pursues, though finding it impossible to reach? "Metamorphosis" relates how love melts a bitterness of soul; "Fall of an Age" cries the protest of a "pawn" in the deadly game played by "masters of war"; "Complexity" shares the poet's conflicted relationship with God in the face of war and other of the world's evils; "Children's Nightmare Rhyme" and "Today" are ironic portraits of evil that will chill adults' blood; E'Val's "Concrete Rose" encourages by showing the tough yearnings of gentle yet indomitable love.

Matters neither little nor great escape the intense yet fervent eye Edward Val casts, with strong tenderness, on our times and the human condition. Prepare as you read to hurt, to weep, to laugh, and superseding all emotion, to think, of the forever in now, with this young man of ancient heart.

Part One:

Spring

A Flicker in the Dark

I walk in the darkness and I know no peace
though I feel the Lord's love with each heartbeat.
So I seek guidance and hope to find
love one day, of a glorious kind.

But today is a day like any other,
I stand alone apart from another
and stare into the darkness I know so well,
remembering my own moments in hell,
recalling the torment, reliving the pain,
wondering how I've remained sane.

Then I remember the light, the brief distant flicker,
and my hope comes alive all the quicker
because I now know *you* were there, calling me home.
So I step forward, my heart no longer alone,
toward something so wonderful and rare:
on toward the arms of that one who cares.

A Silhouette of Beauty

A silhouette of beauty, an angel on the sand,
her mind's lost in wonder, dreaming of distant lands.
She longs for adventure, for things to capture her mind;
she dreams of far-off places and different times.

She's a sight to behold and a treasure to be had,
so curses on those who'd ever make her sad.
She's smart and funny, a goddess in my eyes,
so all praise this angel of beauty who can never die.

A silhouette of beauty, an angel upon the sand,
she's the image of a perfect rose in your hand;
she's like a marble statue, crafted perfectly and strong;
she's a masterpiece painted, a sweetest song.

She's a sight to behold and a treasure to be had,
so curses on those who'd ever make her sad.
She's smart and funny, a goddess in my eyes,
so all praise this angel of beauty who can never die.

Art

Artists create joy:
Romantics praise love and life
to sway the darkness.

Beside Me

I walked the deadliest road I could find,
and there you were beside me;
I climbed the steepest-cragged mountain,
and there you were beside me.
I swam across the rampant oceans,
and there you were beside me;
I flew from earth's one end to the other,
looking for myself, and there you were beside me.
And now, as I walk blindfolded across this tightrope
I can see without looking, since
I know you're here beside me.

Canvas

Beautiful: Endless blue sky overlooking the ocean. Waves crashing on the cliffs. In the distance to the left, you see a castle. To the right, you hear, then see a man approach on a night-black horse. A woman stands near the edge of the cliff, her blue dress fluttering in the breeze, her long brown hair blowing across her face. You see her ruby-red lips, pale-green eyes, white satin ribbons tied in tiny braids in her hair.

The man climbs down from his night-black horse. He comes to the woman and caresses her face. You see in his eyes an endless sea of blue. The world fades around them and disappears as if melting off a canvas.

Locked in an embrace long forgotten, his hand on her cheek, her hand in his hand, they are lost in each other's eyes.

Concrete Rose

To you I still remain unseen,
silently hidden in shadow.
Your eyes never linger
long enough to glimpse me,
yet I am still here; beautiful.

You pass by me every day,
yet never take the time to look – only if you would stop,
you'd surely be amazed.

Long years I have spent here,
struggling to survive,
my determination strong,
my will unwavering; I will make it.

Hopelessness I won't allow to touch me,
nor depression to take hold.
Nothing can make me give up;
I'll never fold.

For I'm the rarest piece of creation,
a winner at the odds; I can't be broken,
not by mortal or by GOD,
for I'm the rose that grew
from concrete, and I shall prevail.

Dear Lord

Dear Lord,
Look at the web I've woven,
so full of deceit and lies.
How can I say I'm your child
when I hold no regret inside,
nor the slightest remorse?

You gave me your warnings,
but I stayed my destructive course;
and at the end there was nothing,
nothing for me to find
but a heart full of emptiness
and punishment for all time.

Why I didn't listen, I really don't know,
but I made friends of my enemies,
and turned friend into foe.

Where to go from this junction?
Not the slightest hint I'm shown,
so I'll continue to walk forward
into the vast unknown,
always searching for a way
back toward your eternal throne.

Dear Wife

Dear Wife,
You've changed my world,
my very simple views:
The black and whites I've always seen
are now violets, reds and blues.

You changed my aspect, my very approach;
the sorrow that once filled my heart diminished –
in its stead now is hope –
then you helped guide me down a far different path
from the one I previously chose.

Now at the end, with you beside me
I'm surely not destined to wilt like a rose;
so I thank you, and may our love always last,
forever into the future drawn
from wondrous memories of our past.

Eternity

Remember the time I kissed your lips
upon a cliff with grass true green? The ocean crashed be-
side us, and the sun set into the sea, orange and red clouds
faded to purple, mauve and blue…

Remember all the things we said, promises of eternity, the
little things, true love and more?
On your knees that night you promised your soul would
love me forever, your mind and heart joined with mine.
You kissed my hands and asked me to live for you alone,
love no other for all time and beyond, a bond between spir-
its, not just hearts.

I never forgot, I still remember the castle by the cliffs,
overlooking the ocean, sun painting the sky.
Love – everlasting like the castle, endless as the ocean, as
true and beautiful as the sky.
Now and for all eternity.

Haiku 1

Today slowly fades
as tomorrow begins to
open its eyes.

I'm Sorry

I'm sorry I can't be there to hold you when you cry;
I'm sorry I can't be there, right now by your side.
I'm sorry you must take care of our son on your own;
I'm sorry you hardly see me, that I'm rarely ever home.
I'm sorry it doesn't always seem like I love you;
I'm sorry the distance makes it so hard.
I'm sorry we're so far apart, our only connection, it seems,
the stars.
I'm sorry for everything I cannot share with, or protect you
from;
I'm sorry that so many times I say, "I've go to run."
I'm sorry baby; I hope you know it's true –
but no matter how many sorries,
remember I'll always love you.

Life Defined

You were born from the earth as all things are,
and one day you will dissolve much like the stars.
Nothing can stop these motions in place;
all one can do is patiently wait;

for the cord has been cut, its length though unknown;
minutes pass as sure as we die alone.
So strive for nothing but happiness, love and peace,
and do the best you can before you cease.

There's only so much time in a day,
and each day quickly flowers, then fades away
into a vast expanse of ever-flowing time,
and nothing can make it stop on a dime.

So with all simplicity take what you're given,
make the best of each moment and get on with living,
for truly our lives are but a flicker in flame,
of hopes, of dreams, of trials and pain.

My Love

My love, you are the
snow of my winter,
the flower of my spring,
the sun of my summer,
the leaf of my fall.
Simply put you're my everything and all:
I love you.

Senryu 1

Newspaper said storm,
severe thunder and lightning:
I see cats and dogs.

Smile

Your smile melts the world,
a perfect piece of sunshine,
uplifting and pure,
that brightens the hearts of all
and our souls within, too.

The Message: Part One

I am lost but not forgotten;
I'm a shining star among so few; I'm the cold touch of
death
that's only felt by those like you.

So as my essence lingers
and I fall victim to a bitter romance,
lend an ear to the darkness,
listen for my voice and your chance,

because beyond these doors lie secrets
trapped in a constant flow of time,
and I'd hate to see you fall tragically
like generations before and mine.

So open your eyes to the world
and learn from each precious lesson,
for history gives us many chances,
and this remains our hope and blessing.

True Beauty

True beauty has finally beset my eyes,
just when I almost gave up
and let my heart die.
Alone and cold inside I felt,
but now the ice has begun to melt
because you give me understanding,
and I thank you.

You take me for who I am;
you don't just want a piece of the pie,
you want the man.
You understand my trials and tribulations
just as I understand yours,
so there's no surprise why
we long for each other
from homeland to foreign shore.

You are the love of my summer, spring, winter and fall;
you are my salvation from the darkness that called.
You are true beauty's definition,
an angel with deep brown eyes;
you are my heart's content that can never die.

Virtues of a Noble Man

In a world of conformity,
I am change.
In a world of pain,
I am love.
In a world of indifference,
I am understanding.
In a world of war,
I am peace.
In a world of questions,
I am the answers.
In a world of disease,
I am a cure.
In a world of misguidance,
I am direction.
In a world of hopelessness,
I am a beacon.
In a world of evil men,
I am the hero.

Warrior of the Light

I feel as though I'm breathing underwater,
my lungs feel so compressed…
I'm tired of fighting all these battles;
I desperately need rest.

Every day I fight
to hold my own against the odds,
battling the demons of dark
as I walk the path of gods,

searching for salvation,
unwavering in my quest,
carrying the many burdens,
each day I meet the test.

And nothing seems to get easier…
every day's full of agonizing pain;
I can feel my strength seeping into
a slow, yet constant drain.

Yet what can I do but fight
until all my power is gone?
Who would I be if I did not struggle
from night to early morn?

Part Two:

Summer

Alas

Long I have fought,
knowing I could never win,
tainted with too much passion
and sin,

though I remain hopeful,
heart always true,
living in daydreams of
me and you.

But it's all for nothing;
you'll never be mine:
An old copper penny
can't court a new dime.

Confused

I stand outside the gates –
won't someone let me in?
I've asked for forgiveness,
tried to cleanse all my sin;
but without you to guide me
I'm destined to fall;
so out here I wonder, confused by it all.

For I've been dropped and shattered,
forgotten and misplaced;
though I carry many burdens,
none among them is hate;
yet, still closed is the gate –
no admittance for one such as me –
the answers to such questions remain a mystery.

So as I walk away, down the only path I know,
through the forest of darkness with its ever-biting cold,
remember that I came seeking forgiveness,
willing to pay my dues,
but the gates stayed unopened,
I was not let through.

What am I to think? What am I to do?
I wander back to where I started,
seeking another route… confused.

Empty Pot

I am but an empty pot,
void and hollow;
nothing fills me,
I am alone.
And like an empty pot,
I am useless
and serve no purpose
on my own.
I need something
to sustain me,
something to nurture me inside; if
not, I might as well crack and die.

I am but an empty pot,
void and hollow;
nothing fills me,
I am alone.
And like an empty pot,
I am useless
and serve no purpose
on my own.
So please give me something,
a reason to be,
because without that
I'm gone: Never again
will you see me.

Fork in the Road

As I stand upon this road
I only ask: Why? Why?
Must this fork divide,
giving me two completely
different selections,
when I know that
after choosing one path
I'm never to know
the other's directions?

Horse and the Fly

I have walked these roads again and again,
longing for love and some I might call friend;
but the paths set before me are hard to endure.
I've walked through brimstone and fire
and still travel burnt shores.
Though I remain faithful, always searching for light,
I'll be damned before I give into the night.
Though the struggle's difficult
(and harder by the day),
I'd burn for all time before I'd give my soul away.

So here I stand overlooking a world of death and decay; all
beauty
has faded; that's why I see things this way.
And nothing will change my view because of what I've
seen:
Darkness engulfs us, with lies seeming ever so clean.
Yet I keep a spark of hope, because I'll never give in.
Yes, I'm far from pure; I'll admit to each of my mortal
sins;
but I'll never sell my soul (that which is I),
and that's the difference between
the horse and the fly.

House of Cards

The fragile house of cards has fallen;
now I'm all alone,
standing with my back exposed to the world,
truly on my own.
With nowhere to go and no place to be,
I live each day free,
though puzzled by the many choices
I try so hard to keep my eyes open to see.
Everything that's possible and life could ever offer,
each single moment of bliss –
I live each day by the moment,
and it's worth standing solo for this.

Life's a Revolving Door

Every day's the same,
nothing ever changes,
just repeats, again and again,

a continuous,
repeating circle
that comes and goes, comes and goes.

Like playing follow-the-leader,
marching to the beat of the same drum,
twenty-four/seven,

there's no exit ramp to freedom,
just bumper-to-bumper traffic
we must follow always,

much as the hands of a clock
make one complete round after another;
we're stuck in the constant round and round,

like the earth we rotate on our axis,
the sun and moon rise and fall,
up and down, up and down…

Every day's the same,
nothing ever changes,
just repeats, again and again…

Maiden to Her Warrior: (Part One)

Warrior, what do you still fight for?
Your enemies are long gone, brought down by your hand;
still, your sword stays by your side,
a dagger up your sleeve,
your weary horse, noble and strong, still weighted with ar-
mor,
fights on with you, far into the night of battles long gone.
A quest you now ride for, you say of endless feats;
you long for love, a gentle touch; to calm your misery.
Warrior, stop your fighting!
No longer search the lands!
Come be my love,
stay by my side, safe
inside my arms!
Let me end your quest – be my love,
love me, as I love you, for eternity!

Warrior to His Maiden: (Part One)

Sweet love, pure as gold,
sadly I cannot venture from my path.
If I but could, I would surely stay by your side forever.
But the task at hand is not yet finished,
and there's one more troubled soul I must free;
if not, then our love can never truly be.
So I beg you to wait; please bide your time, that
one day our true love may shine and breach the
darkness that will torment my heart
once I finish freeing my soul.

Me and You

I leave with a heavy heart:
Every time I say goodbye
it saddens me to see
the tears behind your eyes,
and I hate to bring you pain.

But alas, my love, I must go,
I can't remain;
yet know that I love you;
you fill my every thought;
my heart you've bought.

So don't fret or worry;
soon I'll be home to you.
I only have a few more things to do,
then I'm yours forever, always, true,
till the end of all time, everlasting,
me and you.

Metamorphosis

I live within a darkness
unknown to the light.
I find comfort in the land
of nightmare and fright.

I'm a creature of destruction;
evil is all I know.
My heart is cold and barren;
I've always been alone.

So what do you expect
by beating down my door?
Love is as much a mystery to me
as white sandy shores.

I don't know how to act
in the presence of your grace;
all I know is darkness;
all I breathe is hate.

But I'm starting to feel different,
a slow, steady change within:
My anger is settling,
my heart begins to beat again…

Precious Forever

Her voice, a song carried by the wind;
her eyes, an ocean of endless blue; her
lips, a soft silky peach;
her graceful walk, always a dance;
her face so sweet, so precious…

But all this is long gone; no more do we hear her song; no
longer shall we see the dance of unheard beauty; her eyes
closed, no sea of blue,
un-kissed her lips of true love, lost eternally.
But her face in memory shall stay precious forever.

Reflection

Lost in thought,
pondering

all the choices
made,

distressed by many
reactions…

but the past can't be
changed.

Edward Val

Searching for Answers

I'm a world away from where I started,
and my journey's yet to end.
I've lost and I've gained along the way
when enemies turned friends.

And this land I travel is far different from my own;
it's barren and desolate as I move forward alone
searching for something I couldn't find
where I started, in the land of the living who've yet de-
parted.

And though I search, I still haven't found
the thing I desire most, to which I feel bound;
yet on I continue without stopping, without even pausing
for breath,
because to stop would mean failure, unpleasant death.

So I continue on the path set before me
with no idea where it may lead;
though I've crossed many deserts,
and sailed plentiful seas,

still I've not found what I've been searching for
to make everything so clear;
I haven't found the answers to all my questions,
though I'll never give up, 'cause I know they're so near.

Slaves of Them

The era of the abacus is over;
computers rule today.
No longer is free thought welcome;
we're drones until the grave.

Yes, speech is still "free,"
but "freedom" is also chained;
our Mark Twain's grow fewer
as our rights fly away.

The masses begin to crumble,
caught up in self-loathing.
No one's willing to take a stand,
and thus our world becomes damned.

Injustice, not justice rules here,
iron-gloved and vile,
quick to make an example of anyone
who steps a fraction outside their bounds.

A hundred frowns replace one smile
as our society descends;
no longer free men are we,
but slaves of *them*.

Truth

Truth hides,
      lies we find.
Secrets gone
      but from eyes.

Passion's flown,
      hearts burn.
Time ticks,
      we don't learn.

People sway,
      roads are gone.
Memories stay
      just so long.

Essence dwindles,
      thoughts erase.
Truth evades
      all who chase.

Whispered Warning: (Part One)

Why are we falling, fading further away?
We've lost sight of our roots,
the ground's now all paved,
and today's not today,
just a glimpse of an unforgiving tomorrow.

So do what you can now
before we drown in joyless sorrow,
because life is descending
into darkness without depth;
the world is bleeding –
feel its pain in your chest?

So I beg you
keep fighting, give it your best
before our candle dwindles to nothing,
burnt out like the rest.

Words

Few words escape those
     who've already said so much;
wise words come from those
     who are not far from dust.

Many words leave those
     with youth, enough to forever speak;
loving words escape those
     who seek.

My words echo in darkness,
     heard by but a few
because my words are complex –
     if you only knew…

Part Three:

Fall

Angel Fallen

I'm everything and nothing; I'm
his lost and treasured son; I'm
the begotten and the lonely; I'm
the last and single one.

No words can describe my sorrow
or the pain I've been dealt,
and no soul on earth shall ever know
the anguish I've felt.

For the path chosen was mine alone:
"Prophet of the ages,"
though my hopes and dreams
are now set in stone,
and I've not yet learned a way to set them free,
even with the knowledge he so graciously gave me.

Yet on I continue, trying to find a way,
though the weight I shoulder
grows heavier each day.

As I Live

Even as I live, I'm dying; with each breath, I fade farther
away;
each step carries me closer
to the eternal grave.

Yet I long for the peace I'll find there,
the complete silence of the tomb –
something I've missed
since long before the womb,

because this world I'm not meant for
with its full degrees of pain;
that's why I'm not afraid to die,
and walk peacefully on death's lane,

smiling always,
longing to embrace the end:
Death holds such possibilities;
no need for tears, my friend.

This is the course I've chosen,
where infinite paths wait,
so unlike living,
where emptiness crowds my plate.

So as each minute passes,
counting closer to my demise,
know that I've lived deeply –
but now, time for goodbyes.

Attraction

The pains I feel, the cruelty I see
all go away when you're close to me.
Though it may seem crazy, perhaps even wrong,
these feelings I have for you are that strong.

I can't explain why I feel as I do;
I can only say there's something about you
that strikes me and holds me so near –
it's like stained glass: clear, yet unclear.

But how I feel deep inside, you may never know,
for these things I just cannot show.
I can't ask you to tell me if you feel the same;
too afraid of the answers, my self-doubt's to blame,

so I'll sit here and wonder how deeply you feel
about love's attraction, with heartache too real.

Blind

To many faces of the world
you remain blind,
and some things in the world's darkness
I hope you never find:

Lies by the millions,
heartbreak and deceit,
people who stab in the back,
then act innocent next week.

Some will use you,
make you feel sick,
kick you when you're down
just to get their fix.
Some will steal things
of much value to you –
much more than money or expensive shoes:

For some will take everything,
drain your well dry,
nor care if you die.
So to faces like these I hope you remain blind
and continue to walk where the sun always shines…
forever blind.

Cause and Effect

You walked over me,
        now I feel used;
you blurred my vision,
        left me confused,

pondering thoughts
        not my own,
seeking salvation
        all alone.

So here I stand,
        lost for awhile,
heart grief-filled,
        unable to smile

because you used me,
        destroyed all I knew.
Now I'm nothing…
        because of you.

Complexity

Not far now,
just a few steps away,
I'm calling on you, Lord,
please help me be saved
from this world so full of sin
before my destruction begins.

Because I'm too weak, no longer strong,
and all I do now seems so wrong,
please O Lord, bless me,
hold me to your chest;
I've seen so many of my brothers fall,
and I fear for the rest
as I wonder
if there's a point behind this madness
as bullets fired, end in pain:
War begets war, will it ever change?
Or shall we remain deranged,
thinking war will bring about peace,
when, after all the battles ever fought,
war has yet to cease?

Or are we just too simple-minded
in the complexity of it all?
Are we not more beasts than men,
designing our own downfall?
So I ask for an answer to the questions I seek –
or are we doomed to sow always
that which we must reap?

Disposed

The candle that was is nevermore;
      heart's been torn away,
tossed to the floor,
      waiting to be stepped on
and crushed to tiny bits,
      all because you broke me
beyond any fix.
      I loved you, I meant each syllable,
sound, constant and vowel;
      these meant nothing to one heartless as you,
and that's why I'm now merely
      disposed of after use.

Fall of an Age

It's easy to send pawns to war when
you're sitting on high as king.
But when the rooks and knights forever rest
the pendulum begins its downward swing.

Then, when the bishop tragically falls
and mortality begins to sing,
you sit and ponder what you've done
as the alarm bells ring.

You pull your queen beside you
and helplessly cling
as the death-blow comes nearer...
checkmate for the king.

Fate

I was born to this world
and one day will be erased.
So is this that
great thing they call
Fate?

From Myself to Myself

I cry real tears, while your eyes are dry.
I run from fears; you hold none inside.
I fear to see myself and all I've become;
you show no remorse for what you've done.

You're everything I hate, I'm all you despise.
You're one I can't stand; I'm one you wish would die.
I struggle every day, you long to say goodbye.
But one of us without the other would be only half a whole;
So until the end of days, we'll battle for control.

Haiku 2

Rose petals falling,
bittersweet song sung:
death has come calling.

I Dare Not

I dare not put into words
the way you make me feel,
for fear of rejection and its sad appeal.

I dare not shed light on my emotions,
for rejection is a vast and lonely ocean.

I dare not hint toward a meaning
for all the things I do,
because I might risk losing you.

I dare not, so I will not,
and never shall *we* be.

Illusion

Standing beside myself,
lost somewhere between
    love and hate,
I don't quite understand our situation,
and I'm unable to digest what's
    been thrown on my plate.

Because yesterday everything was fine,
then in a blink it all changed:
We went from laughter and love
    to hatred and pain.

And you say it's my fault,
but I could always tell when you lied.
You're hiding some dark secret,
yet I can see the truth behind your eyes.

But does it really matter?
Truth be told, I don't really care,
because I realize now that I always loved you,
but you were never really there:
Our love was but a figment of imagination;
    a particle in air.

Image

Lying in bed, his hand stretched out,
subconsciously seeking the person who once slept beside
him
without luck,
only his dreams comfort him, the memories of better days
and what used to be.
He tries not to wake, as he fights off the world because the
truth
is too much to bear.
As his feelings tear at him so,
heartbroken and alone he prefers to live in his dreams
rather than face reality with all its anguish.
He'd rather give up and forget life than deal with the
pain…
of having lost her.

In a Fallen World

I live in a world of devastation
where death always circles so near;
I live in a world of destruction
where the truth remains unclear.

So where in this world does hope live –
or has it already died?
Where in this world is there peace,
or is it just another lie?

I live in a world of chaos;
pain is always close at hand;
I live in a world of confusion;
answers are always in demand.

So where in this world does hope live –
or has it already died?
Where in this world is there peace,
or is it just another lie?

I live in a world of sadness
that drains the soul of man;
I live in a world of seduction
that takes from god's great plan.

So where in this world does hope live –
or has it already died?
Where in this world is there peace,
or is it just another lie?

I live in a world that's fading
faster with each breath;
I live in a world that's fallen
close to living death.

In His Name

You're the master of manipulation,
you made me feel things that were never there.
You turned what could have been love
into something untruthful and unfair.

You unraveled my coils
and just let me fray.
You turned the once beautiful world I saw
passionless and gray.

You destroyed my youthful spirit,
turned me against those I loved.
You took away my very innocence
the moment you covered my hands in blood.

Now you wonder why I'm this demon,
a monster even you can't control?
It's because you destroyed me,
took what once made me whole.

So now my every thought is sinister,
and destruction follows in my wake.
Feel the wrath of your creation
as the world starts to violently shake,

for I am he who has come
to punish all who against me stand:
with sword and cleansing fire
I will craft and reshape the land,

molding a new paradise from the ashes
so none shall ever again feel alone,
bridging gaps that need much mending
on this earth we once called home.

Inside Me

I feel it, it's there every day
inside me, slowly eating away.
I cannot describe it, this thing deep inside;
it hurts me and rules me, by it I abide.
It cuts like a knife through my flesh to my bone;
with no one to turn to, I face it alone.
It tells me to do things, to make me forget,
so I do as it says, always to my regret.
A slice here, a burn there – no one will see
this thing that's inside, slowly destroy me.
I feel it, it's there every day
inside me, slowly eating away…

Life/Death

Life:
New, Fresh,
Breathing, Living, Loving,
Wonderful, Enjoyable, Painful, Unpleasant,
Suffering, Dying, Ending,
Dead, Gone:
Death.

Love Is...

Love is a gateway to destruction,
> a pathway to a broken heart.
Love is a road of sacrifice,
> a way that can tear you apart.
Love is pain in many forms,
> a question you can't answer.
Love is never-ending torment,
> a plague like cancer.
Love is vile and crude,
> and love is often untrue,

But…

Love is also a door to passion,
> a cure for the emptiness inside.
Love is a wonderful union,
> linking two souls side by side.
Love is blissful existence,
> powerful and wondrous romance.
Love is sharing feelings
> in a long exquisite trance.
Love is caring and love is kind,
> and true love is always there to find.

Edward Val

Oh, Heart of Mine

Has my heart yet again led me down a broken road,
one all too familiar and unpleasantly cold –
or has it just selected for me
another rotten apple in my never-ending battle
for a key to my heart?
Truth be told, I can't take it any longer,
and my world's already falling apart.

So please I beg you, oh, heart of mine,
close your broken gate,
bar it shut, secured with chain, keep out the pain
before it's too late,
for my world's crumbling,
and I can't handle another quake.
Numb to the world I am,
and all I'm holding onto is about to break.

So, oh, heart of mine – I beg you:
Lock yourself away;
I'm tired of playing, I'm tired of trying
and always getting the same.
This is it, it's over,
this is it, I'm done.
The noose is drawn up;
my lonely heart's hung.

One Last Question

Everything has been broken;
sharp pieces of glass now litter the ground.
The world I once knew is falling apart, the walls are com-
ing down.
Why did you have to leave and turn my life so black?
Why did you have to walk away and never come back?
Didn't I give you everything? I sacrificed in every way.
What made you so unhappy? Why'd you go away?
I still don't understand it, as I sit here confused.
One last question:
Must I have lost everything when I lost you?

Paper Tears

The hurt in his eyes isn't easy to read:
Walks on, stands tall, head held high,
no reaction, no defense,
just a solemn face.

But through the door in his Sanctuary
true emotions you can read
with every line, every letter, each unspoken word.

Why is he the mime, why not a voice to be heard except
on paper, hidden elsewhere, no feelings to show,
paper tears, never fallen
on one who'll ever know?

Rant

Razor blades slice through skin like paper.
So all I see is a river red,
everything seems to be spinning,
I'm knocking on the door:
Please, I beg, let me be dead,
'cause life gives me no comfort,
no smiles nor joys.
I long for happiness,
but it's always on the other side
of a bottomless void.

So please, I beg, let me bleed out,
let it all be over soon,
I don't know how much longer I can survive
looking at all the memories in our old room.
I need to get away, and suicide seems faster;
maybe I'll meet you in the after-
life; I'm going to hell, and you're coming with me
'cause you brought on this disaster.

But don't fret; it's not solely you I blame;
I blame the one who stole you, and hope he lives in pain.
So as the brimstone rains and your world dissolves in fire,
I hope you can find happiness… walking barefoot on
barbed wire.

Silent Pain, Silent Plead

The silent pain took her, as it had so many before,
the moment she chose to close that door.
You couldn't see it, but only in her eyes
because she chose to live in lies.
Though she wept many tears, clawed
at the haunted walls year after years,
nothing could change the fact that he'd passed.
But she begged and pleaded with the Lord, until at last
he granted her wish and gave her release:
She saw her husband once again and knew true peace.

Edward Val

Silently

Standing on the brink of damnation,
　all my bridges burned, silently
　　waiting for it to be my turn,

long I have stood here
　　　frozen in place,
silently remembering, all the times of hate,

understanding
　　　that nothing can be done,
silently missing each and everyone;

but this fate I've chosen,
　　　no one else to blame, silently
hating the fact I couldn't change;

so here I stand in judgment,
　　　awaiting the decree,
silently hoping you've not forsaken me;

though knowing I deserve no forgiveness,
　　　not the slightest reprieve,
silently needing something to believe;

for long ago I fell,
　　　consumed by desire and greed,
silently searching for what I need;

thus I became misguided,
　　　selfish thoughts all my own,
silently traveling into the vast unknown

with no slightest direction,
　　　vacant of light,
silently seeking a way through the night.

The Message: Part Two

Stop the hating, put your differences aside –
too much violence plagues the world,
so throw away your guns and knives!
Use your voice to make a difference,
rise together and make a stand –
strength is found in numbers,
so form a chain, hand in hand.
Alone in this world, you cannot make it;
like wet paper you'll easily break;
but rise together, like birds in flight.
You're clueless as the earth begins to shake,
so take solace in all you've been given;
rise up and make a change
before it's too late, and the world drowns
in its own ignorance and pain.

Unanswered

I walk all alone on the darkest of nights;
I look for the answers, I search for the light.
I search on for hours, the question so clear,
through seas of confusion with no answers near

and with no one to guide me, to show me the way.
Every step's a mistake, for which I'll eternally pay;
so I ask for the answers, I plead for just one.
Show me the path to the light of the sun!

Yet my questions aren't answered – is this how it shall stay
as fear and much sorrow take my life away?

We're Through

I can't walk on eggshells
in a world you love and I despise.
And how can I tell the truth when all you give me are lies?
And how can I speak my mind,
when you try to control my tongue?

Gasping for air, I feel as though I'm slowly being hung,
so how am I supposed to enjoy my freedom
when I get none from you?
I feel like a breath of air,
uncared for but always used.
You make me so miserable, I can't remember
when last I smiled.

My thoughts are always on the future;
yours are like an immature child's;
somehow it's always about you.
You care nothing for others, you simply use,
and I'm tired of being a tool in your kit, just an end to a
means.

So from this day forth, I'll remain unseen, because
I don't need this, or anything you do –
we're over my darling; that's right, we're through.

Part Four:

Winter

A Soldier's Tears

Perplexing thoughts still linger
as I hang onto but a thread.
I've tried all my days to avoid this ending,
but couldn't prevent being doom-led,
and nothing said seems to fix
the great damage done,
and sadly, hurt and pain can't easily be undone;
it seems I've ran out of places to run.

So with a weakening grasp I turn
to face my fate, to abolish my fears,
and to ask forgiveness for all I've done over the years
as I cry a soldier's tears.

After a Bride's Death

Staring out the window, lost in memories,
no one gives much comfort to one such as he.
His home's dark and forbidding;
it's long since he's let another in.
Old pictures hang on the walls, as his tears fall
with thoughts of what could have been.

He looks not forward to old age or the days to come;
he cares only for the past and his bottle of rum.
His thoughts fix on the days when he held her close;
those times he misses the most.

He doesn't dare think of when she was taken away,
for to him that was the most tragic of days.
He stares out the window, remembering what was:
The shower of flowers and the woman he loves.

Bedside Farewell

Dead I shall be come the morning light,
but for now let us enjoy this dark, splendid night.
For I love you in so many different ways –
if only I could hold you once again in the sun's
warm rays.

But sadly, I am fading, faster then I wish,
so grant me the pleasure, my love, of just one more
kiss.
Then walk away – I couldn't bear to see the tears
you'd cry.
I've loved you always; I'll love you even after I die

So as I slip away from this world into the next,
know that because I had you I'll be happy as I rest.
You were my everything, my bright evening star;
so when you grow lonely, look up, I'll be twinkling
afar…
      always there to love you, distant though you
are.

Broken Stones

Lying here bleeding, thoughts all my own,
I long to repair our broken home, stone by stone.
But you destroyed everything, you took it all,
so with one last slice, to eternal darkness I fall.

Children's Nightmare Rhyme

I walk in stealth and shadow;
my passing goes unknown,
silent as a falling feather;
my skill is world renowned.

I'm deadly as a viper,
cunning beyond my years;
my work is quickly done;
in my wake flow tears.

None know my true name,
but their whispers I hear;
I am death's champion;
I cause nothing but fear.

My blade is always sharp;
I can strip flesh from bone.
I come late at night –
beware when you're alone.

Damaged

Destroyed beyond repair,
annihilation complete,
monstrous now to behold,
asymmetrically formed,
grotesque in appearance,
estranged from all others…
damaged for good.

Death

Another day, another death
I hold under my breath,
one last chance
to gasp for air,
for I and this world
just don't care.

Death Is...

Death is
hard, cold, final.
Death is
despair.
Death is
a poison.
Death is
here, there, everywhere.
Death is
darkness.
Death is
a tunnel bare of light.
Death is
eternal beauty.
Death is
the eternal night.

Downward Spiral

Circling, circling
round and round,
sinking further
down and down

deep into darkness
empty of light,
to depths untouched
by even the night;

deeper we fall
into nothing, its true,
pealing back the pure shell
that sheltered us two;

as death takes his hold
and the world starts to burn,
shock scars faces of all
who find it their turn,

until nothing remains
except for a void:
This road we have followed
till all's been destroyed.

Edward Val

Empty and Bitter

Empty and bitter,
I dare not move a step.
I know I have no choice but to live,
though I'd rather give up and take my rest.
Life is so complicated,
all ups and downs;
I'm tired of seeing smiles
while I can only frown.
Nothing ever seems to go my way;
resistance fights me pound for pound,
so how, concrete-shoed, am I not to drown?

Or is this supposed to be some test,
a rite of passage, if you like,
where answers will be given that I've sought all my life –
or am I to find the same emptiness I've always found
in this world of man, with no hallowed ground?
I say I can't take it
if what I guess is true:
You see, I've always aimed to win,
but all I ever do is lose.

So how can I believe your divine words today,
when they'll only bring me heartbreak tomorrow?
Is it not better to live in the world I know,
this one of bitterness and sorrow,
rather than be torn apart by the love of lovers,
come tomorrow?

Haiku 3

Great gaps divide us
even to this very day:
Your touch forgotten.

Haiku 4

Drooping, falling down,
slowly turning red to brown:
Petals on the ground.

I tried

The roses are dead now,
all thanks to me,
not you.

Once bright red roses,
now black
as hell's depths.

I tried to give you a better
life,
but I tripped and
all the roses fell.

They never made it to your
home
and the water they needed,
so their surviving strength
depleted.

And now your once bright
red roses
turn black
as I die.

In Memory of T.J., a Soldier

Sadly another star has fallen, one
more soldier set under stone, life
taken, laid to rest,
because with pride and honor he protected his home.

He was brave, his life he gave defending a cause.
He'll always be remembered, for sacrifice never to out-
weigh the loss.
He was a man, a brother, a soldier, a friend
who would stand beside you until the end.

So he'll not be forgotten, his memory will always remain
even as his coffin's draped in red, white, blue and your
pain.
Think only to remember one once like you,
and pray that god takes him with open arms…
and know he's in a better place now, far from
harms.

In Remembrance

Thousands of lives lost:
The ultimate cost
paid in full by the most valiant groups,
the young, ever fearless, fighting troops.

Edward Val

Let Me Go, I'm Tired

So full of love, yet so alone,
I'm like rust on a throne of bone.
I don't belong, I don't fit in,
I'm a secret kept
yet carried on wind.

In truth,
I'm the black star hidden in the night sky;
I'm the silent shadow that lurks by.
I'm the one chosen to both live and die;
I'm the one who can't shed tears while others cry.
So why not just let me go, let me fade away;
I serve no further purpose, and I'm tired of being "saved."

Why must you insist on my survival?
Don't give me, "You're in denial,"
for I know who I am:
Long ago I was banished to this distant land, and
nowhere along the path are my boot-prints
absent from the sand, nor does he hold my hand.

So I ask again: Why must I remain?
Just let me go, tired of being a stain.
Weary of all the pain, torment and lies,
I'm tired of the deceit the lies behind your eyes.
I just want to go away, to escape this place,
and find somewhere understanding, empty of hate.

Man

You're the most destructive force on earth;
you're the greatest power the world has ever known.
You've conquered lands and vanquished kings; you've
razed cities until they were all but forgotten.
You've mastered the art of killing and do it for sport;
you've betrayed allies and broken bread with enemies.
You've watched men, women and children murdered;
you've laughed and joked about their cries of pain.
You've raped and pillaged, lied and stolen;
you've brought about the death of millions.
You're a living plague upon the land.
You are man.

Our Red, White and Blue

As day transcends to night and night to day,
remember those who fought the battle
but didn't survive the fray:
They're the ones who ensure our freedom,
high though the price to pay.
They're the ones who walk through hell,
knowing all along it might be their last day.

So never forget those who've fallen,
whose spirits have gone away,
for if not for their sacrifice
our freedom might stray
and our red, white and blue
turn deep, depressing gray.

Struggle

Have I been captured and severely tortured,
trapped and locked away?
My inner voice is screaming,
but my body has nothing to say.

Damnation I feel is rising
as the world turns black and gray;
the sun's no longer smiling;
it says goodbye and fades forever away.

So misfortune alone now guides us,
lies are all they speak;
nothing can change our plight;
the strong prevail, destroying the weak.

All I see is brimstone and fire,
a shell of what used to be;
yet I know that despite the chaos and havoc
I still won't let you consume me or have your fill.

I'd rather burn for all time than give in to your will;
and that's what sets me apart, why alone I stand:
why you're still a boy, and I'm already a man.

Today

I'm the shell of a man,
a demon in disguise.
I've fallen from above,
but from the fires I shall rise
to strike fear into the world
and set it afire –
I'm a thief in the night,
a soul collector and liar.

I was born from total darkness,
raised to hate the light;
I am death by many names;
you're my enemy to fight.
So say farewell to those you love,
you'll never see them again:
I'm a destroyer of worlds,
and yours is at its end.

So pray all you want;
it'll do you little good.
Cower before me,
fear me, for you should:
I'm the executioner
the great taker of lives
and sadly, today
is the day *you* die.

True Love

True love is a myth
with no form of conception,
a whisper on wind,
an unlearnable lesson;
nonexistent, with no place in our world,
true love is a fairy tale
for little boys and girls.

True love's painful to pursue,
impossible to find,
like digging for treasure
above a land mine.
True love's a lie,
rotten, bitter to all,
the unreachable summit
from whom all will fall.

It's the endless battle
to win a broken heart; true
love is a deception that
rends and tears apart.
Most evil of things,
as deadly as dark, it's
devoid of feeling,
a pointless journey better not to embark.

True love is a trick
that cannot exist,
yielding only pain to find.
It's the dead cold of winter
with no thaw in sight;
it's the path to a heart
absent of all light.

Unsaved

The struggle within has me baffled
as disillusioned dreams become my only friends
in this world of madness without ends;
and it's in this world of madness
I've chosen to roam
'cause no peace could I find
where I once used to call home.
So on my own I survive day by day,
careful every moment,
watching each card cautiously played.
I know I should have left long ago,
but I hold no regrets because I stayed,
though the world shifts from light to darkness
and my soul remains unsaved.

Vampire

Pulsing, pumping
through your veins,
I hear your blood calling,
calling out my name.

Each heartbeat brings you
closer to being drained;
I don't know how long
I can withstand the pain
or hold back the frightful
change.

So run while I still
remember your name,
run to keep us both sane.
Again, I hear your blood call-
ing,
calling out my name

War

Wondrously wicked,
Absolutely traumatic,
Repentance a must

Where I Walk

Where I walk death follows,
striking fear into the hearts of men.
Only those who doubt not life
shall survive till the greater end.
So I beg you, do not fall
or you'll risk losing all:
He, the dark specter,
my companion at odds,
hoists a toast in your favor,
to your slumbering nods.

You can follow Edward Val at:

www.lostsoulzpress.com

www.ingramcontent.com/pod-product-compliance
Lightning Source LLC
Chambersburg PA
CBHW070547030426
42337CB00016B/2389